"IMAGE IS EVERYTHING!"
What Does Your Image Say About You?

StudioSteffanie Wealth & Wellness Coach
863 Flat Shoals Rd #139
Conyers, GA 30094
678.330.8139
StudioSteffanie@gmail.com

www.StudioSteffanie.com

Steffanie Haggins, founder/director of StudioSteffanie Enterprises, Inc.

Quotes by StudioSteffanie

"Love doesn't hurt, it helps!"

"Self-Esteem – No one is born with it but you can't live a successful life without it."

"Beauty comes from within. You can't purchase it at the local retail store."

"Success has little to do with possession of material things. Success has everything to do with what's within. Are you truly successful?"

"Take an initiative to discover what your true passion is."

"Depend upon yourself for happiness, not the opinions of others for your joy."

"A Diva will have haters; that just comes with the territory."

"Stop and take time to analyze what you think about."

"There's joy and/or pain associated with your choices, but you must decide."

"Life is like an uncompleted jigsaw puzzle. All the pieces are there, if you could just see the complete picture."

"Having control of your life means that your mind, body, and spirit are working harmoniously."

"IMAGE IS EVERYTHING!"
What Does Your Image Say About You?

<u>DEDICATION</u>

I dedicate this work to our Creator first and next to my wonderful children: Kia, Erica, and Jabari whom I love dearly and appreciate their love, patience, and assistance…

This book is also dedicated to all of the people that read this book and apply the quality time it takes to complete this workbook while pursuing your dreams and aspirations for success!

Steffanie Haggins, also known as *StudioSteffanie*, has long held a passion for wanting to see people in their best image, which ultimately starts with a high self-esteem. It started while she

was being raised in Chicago by her father, who knew nothing about how to groom and care for a young lady. He knew he wanted the best outcome for her future. Therefore, he enrolled her in private schools and into various charm schools and modeling schools; any and every organization that could assist her in becoming a beautiful young lady, internally as well as externally.

Throughout the years *StudioSteffanie* has witnessed and experienced the extraordinary benefits of being introduced to the rules of proper etiquette, speaking, and walking confidently and taking care of oneself to the best of their ability mentally, physically, and spiritually.

StudioSteffanie further cultivated her passion for inspiring others and motivating them to be the best they can be while she was searching for her true passion in life, (a true entrepreneur) which is helping others help themselves become the best they can be. Of course, this sounds cliché; however, it's very sincere. This has been observed over the years while *StudioSteffanie* has assisted models, actors, and independent artists. "I consult with them to discover their true talent and begin to assist in branding their image to prepare them for a global economy." *StudioSteffanie*

She currently works with everyone from celebrities to politicians to the general public at large. "There are no boundaries for true inspiration and motivation. Unfortunately there are people everywhere you turn that are truly unhappy with themselves. They can have all the money and other materialistic items needed to make a person smile; however, they can't truly smile until self-esteem is prevalent."

StudioSteffanie Agency was created in 2009 out of a necessity to help the younger generations especially get a head start in life by acquiring the knowledge needed to instill strong self-esteem. In order to excel in whatever goal(s) you want to accomplish, having high self-esteem helps a person no matter what road in life they choose to take. This agency was created as a "safe haven" for people searching for true assistance, without being taken advantage of. She further fostered this passion by creating workshops that cover topics such as: learning the value of self, basic principles of etiquette, hygiene, the importance of a great education, how to handle stress, self-image, responsibility, peer pressure, choices, even branding, marketing, and business plans. With the completion of her latest workshops, you become a certified Diva gaining independence and feeling great! "As an image consultant, I created this workbook from the best advice I've received throughout my lifetime of achievements, mistakes, experiences, and adventures. This book is for Divas that want the best life has to offer them and are willing to apply the necessary action to accomplish their goals. You can contact me at StudioSteffanie@gmail.com."

Table of Contents

Chapter One
Self-Image Assessment:

Chapter Two
The Elegance of Femininity:

Chapter Three
Knowing Your Self-Worth:

Chapter Four
There's an Art to Being Smart:

Chapter Five
You Must Get Fit:

Chapter Six
Mastering Self-Control:

Chapter Seven
Accepting Self-Responsibility:

Chapter Eight
The Dangers of Mind-Altering Substances:

Chapter Nine
Employee v. Self-Employed:

Chapter Ten
The Life of a True Diva:

"Image Is Everything!"
What does your image say about you?

Instructional Approach:

This is a self-learning workbook that inspires and supports a series of needs that every girl needs to know for your mind, body, and soul; which equals inner peace of mind and a balanced lifestyle. This workbook is your action plan. You will be able to see yourself and your world improve through this journal and your journey throughout your lifetime! Through your learning process, pass the knowledge forward to others. There will be some questions for you to complete at the end of each chapter, and I strongly encourage you to date your submissions within this book to see your advancement over time.

What this Self-Help Workbook Achieves:

- Building self-esteem and less dependency
- Learning the power of your thoughts
- Guiding and gaining control of your emotions
- Improving your overall image – for the mind, body, and soul
- Improving your skills socially, behaviorally, and academically
- Knowing what works best for you financially as an employee or being self-employed
- Learning what it takes to be a **"Diva"**

Essential Terminology

Self-Esteem: **(n.) A realistic respect for or favorable impression of oneself; self-respect.**
Example: "The President has a high level of self-esteem."

Diva: **(n.) A glamorous and successful female performer or personality.**
(n.) A Diva is a female version of a hustler. (*Beyoncé*)
Example: "StudioSteffanie is definitely a Diva!"

Gold Digger: **(n.) A person who has not discovered the talents they truly possess and choose to use and/or destroy people for their personal gain.**
Example: "Don't date or marry a gold digger. You'll regret it later."

Hater(s): **(n.) A person who has a very low self-esteem about themself and tries to pretend that they like themselves but they don't. Then, they will try to make you believe you want to be like them, but they don't buy it either.**
Example: "I won't let those haters affect my happiness."

Man: **(n.) An adult male person, as distinguished from a boy or a woman.**
Example: "He is such a distinguished looking man."

Woman: **(n.) An adult female person.**
Example: "She is a sophisticated young woman."

Chapter One

Self-Image Assessment!

Chapter Summary:
This chapter is designed to teach you the importance of a high self-esteem, the power of thought through words, and preparation for your future. It is designed to teach you how to discover the purpose for your life, create tasks, and complete goals. This chapter also discusses the importance of sharing with others. You are encouraged to take the self-analysis assessment at the end each chapter and discover ways in which you can improve your weaknesses. You will also learn the benefits of knowing the power of thoughts and how negative and positive thoughts can set the pace for your successes and/or failures throughout life.

> *Statistics Show: American girls suffer the most from eating disorders, low self-esteem, and depression.*

Self-Image: (n.) The idea, conception, or mental <u>image</u> one has of oneself.

This chapter will help you:

➤ <u>Effectively zero in on elevating your self-esteem</u>

It may take some people time to zero in on who they really are but the beautiful thing about life is that you have time to learn. Why do you exist here on this planet? This is where you think about why you are here, what you want to accomplish and how you want to contribute to society while you are still alive. As a child I always dreamt of driving in my hot two-seater convertible and parking into my high-rise condo right over Lake Michigan. All I needed to figure out was how I can make that a reality for my future as an adult. What education was needed for me to financially support myself, but first I needed to figure out what I wanted to do for a living.

So, what is the purpose of your life? If you are not sure, one technique that you can use to figure it out is to write a list of what you truly like to do and what you definitely don't want to do. In your journal list everything you like about yourself starting from the top of your head to the bottom of your feet. I'm sure there is something that sets you apart from everyone else. If you have beautiful features, you can become a model or if you have pretty hands and feet, you can model for magazines especially with beautiful hair. Now that's just some of your physical traits; what about the personality traits that you have, what do you like most? Some people are very intelligent, very outgoing and friendly, goal oriented, etc. Now, with all of this information available for you to see yourself, you can get an idea of who you are and what makes your day seem brighter. Observe your list and think of all the potential careers associated with the things you like to do.

Once you understand who you are and what direction you are going in life, even if it's only a temporary goal, you can better accomplish your goals now because you have direction. Knowing where you're going in life gives you inner confidence to know that you can create tasks to achieve goals and create your destiny in a financially safe and positive manner.

➤ Seek positive qualities and eliminate excuses

A great way to filter your thoughts on where you excel and where you "lack" is to figure out where you are in life now. Are you happy? Are you sad? Are you neutral? Do you care? Are you working towards a goal and meeting your deadlines with your tasks? What do you like to do and where do you like to go, and who you like to associate yourself with all need to be considered when you are observing who you are and if you need improvement; and if so where? It is a fact that the people you associate yourself with are a direct reflection of where you are mentally. In other words, are your friends crazy? If so, you may need to take a long and serious look at yourself. It is useful to associate with people who are smarter than you are because they are usually able to handle tasks and complete them without too many excuses. Excuses <u>sound</u> good but hold you back from progress.

What are some of the positive qualities you possess and how do you plan to maximize your opportunities with those talents and skills? The more beneficial your skills and talents are for your financial success, the less you have to worry about depending upon others. Make sure to take some time to think about any negative tendencies you may have and eliminate them immediately because they only hold you back from your success.

➤ Learn the power of thought through words

When a loved one expresses their feelings of love to you, it strengthens you. If someone gossips about you, will you allow it to tear you apart? Emotions are attached to our thoughts. Your mind is a collection of your thoughts. Do you possess *stinking thinking*? This book is *<u>all about you</u>!* Do you ever analyze what you think about? Are you a positive or negative thinker? You are a collection of your genetic makeup, experiences, environments, and thoughts. We need to start here and see how you view yourself. What comes to mind when you think of yourself? Do you have a positive mindset or a negative one? Some positive attributes can include: intelligence, peaceful, insightful, humorous, sweet, strong, determined, classy, beautiful, loving, etc. Some negative attributes can include: small, weak, timid, shy, ugly, dumb, ignorance, stank, poor, etc.

Whatever your environmental circumstances are does not necessarily reflect who you are as an individual. You need to determine how you want to feel about yourself and what you want to accomplish and how you want to live throughout this process. Once you have determined your decisions on how you want to live your life, now it's time to work on your perception – which should be positive – and learning and understanding the power of your thoughts. There is power in your words. And your words come from your thoughts. If you want to think you are doomed, well you will be doomed, eventually. If you want to create a legacy, how would you think to think? Here's a simple thought on how to think: if you accept positive thoughts, it empowers you; if you carry negative thoughts, it will drain you.

You have the power to reject negative thoughts and create positive habits. From time to time it may seem as though your mind wants to play tricks with you and you may start to think negatively about yourself and you start to doubt who you are and what you're made of. Always remember that everyone has moments when they may have doubts about their ability to accomplish a task, even experts. It's wise to remember that as soon as that negative thought comes into your head, you have the power to remove it immediately!

➢ <u>Develop Goals: short, intermediate, and long term</u>

Great news! Hopefully, we have to live for a long, long time; therefore, you should have a road map to help guide your direction. You need to create your own personal map to prepare you for *your* future. If you can, take some time out and look at one of your pictures when you were a baby or toddler. Speak to that little child and reassure her that you won't let her down. You will do your best to have a balanced life and peace of mind.

Once you determine what your future holds and have made your mind up (for this moment in time) that is your goal. Now, it's time to determine what is needed to complete your short-term, intermediate, and long-term goals. Write them down and stick to it. This is a great way to just get started. This information can be written in your journal in pencil until you know for certain which direction you will start. It is essential to date all of your entries and create dates for your goals, too. If your plans are to become a doctor, that would be considered a long-term goal. Then you need to create an intermediate goal, which could be to work temporary jobs until you accomplish your doctor's degrees. An example of a short-term goal would be to ask yourself what's needed immediately in order to survive comfortably until you can accomplish your long-term goals.

➢ <u>Create a purposeful life and share with others</u>

Life is meant to be enjoyed individually and collectively with others through friends, family, and associates. Your life can be full of joy and delight if you purposefully make right decisions and choices throughout your life. We have to survive and strive in life, but why can't you enjoy living life every day? Yes, negative issues may arise that are beyond your control; however, you stay focused on your goals in life and remember to practice prayer, patience and persistence. Determine early in life how you would like to contribute to society comfortably and in the process of reaching your goals, bless others along the way. You will gain an inner peace while assisting others when you're able to do so.

➢ <u>Develop a strategy to achieve goals and create your plans for success</u>

What I have discovered that works for me is to sit back, undisturbed, and envision what the specific goal is that needs to be accomplished. Now, you must determine how much time you have to meet that particular deadline. What all is needed for the project? Is it possible to achieve the goal of that specific task after you see everything involved? List everything. If so, get your calendar and start making plans to complete your task(s) and stick to it. If you're not able to achieve the goal after looking at everything, then simply look at other possibilities on how to handle the situation or create something entirely different and start the planning process over again.

Don't be afraid to look in the mirror and get to know yourself on a more personal basis. In order to recognize what you want to accomplish, you must know who you are and where you want to go. Once the list has been completed of your dos and don'ts, you should also include your desires and timelines. Make sure it's obtainable. You can make it happen!

SELF – ANALYSIS
Assessment

Chapter 1

1. Who are you?

   _____
   _____
   _____
   _____
   _____

2. What makes you unique?

   _____
   _____
   _____
   _____
   _____

3. Do you like yourself or have a different opinion of yourself? Please explain.

   _____
   _____
   _____
   _____
   _____

4. How do your morals and standards, that have guided your life so far, influence your life?

   _____
   _____
   _____
   _____
   _____

5. What are the some of the activities you enjoy most? Why?

_____
_____
_____
_____
_____

6. What are some of your greatest achievements?

_____
_____
_____
_____
_____

7. What challenges are you currently facing?

_____
_____
_____
_____
_____

8. What are your short-term plans (6 months to 3 years from now)?

_____
_____
_____
_____
_____

9. What are your long-term plans (3 years and beyond)?

_____
_____
_____
_____
_____

10. Identify your major strengths.

_____

_____

_____

_____

_____

11. What plans do you have prepared to maximize your potential in life?

_____

_____

_____

_____

_____

12. Identify what areas of your life need improvement.

_____

_____

_____

_____

_____

13. How can you transform these areas of improvement into action?

_____

_____

_____

_____

_____

14. What powerful words can you add to your vocabulary and start expressing them as well?

_____

_____

_____

_____

_____

15. What are some other ways you can truly break your bad habits and create good habits?

_____

_____

_____

_____

_____

16. What or who inspires you?

_____

_____

_____

_____

_____

17. How does the opinion of others make you feel?

_____

_____

_____

_____

_____

18. What do you believe is your "calling" or what is your purpose in life?

_____

_____

_____

_____

_____

Chapter Two:

The Elegance of Femininity:

Chapter Summary:
This chapter is designed to teach the importance of embracing womanhood. Learn to love being a woman and accepting all of the benefits and responsibilities that go along with it; such as, how to communicate effectively, stand tall, sit properly, and have an overall look of confidence that compliments elegance. It's important to know basic etiquette rules as a Diva. Know what to do in a difficult situation with dignity. Learn how to properly apply makeup and have healthy skin.

> *Statistics Show: Most girls believe they don't look good without purchasing a product to enhance their beauty.*

Femininity: (n.) The quality of being <u>feminine</u>; womanliness. **2. W**omen collectively.

This chapter will help you:

> ➤ <u>Understand the responsibility of being a woman</u>

The power of womanhood, there's nothing else like it. A man will fight wars and work hard to find that special woman *(or women)* to keep his company and to bear his children. People live for your love. Life begins through woman. This is the most honored position to be in as a woman – Embrace it!

Who are your role models? Analyze who you are and think of ways in which you can create the best *you* possible. You have the choice and power to create your own destiny. Choose the best people to associate yourself with in your inner circle of friends and feel free so you can thrive throughout life. Don't live life half way – go all the way! Your future is not just finding a job and paying bills; it is living and loving your life. You have plenty of years to live; therefore, live life in the best way possible for you. Maximize your opportunities. And remember a woman must maintain a respectful disposition throughout her journey. The beauty associated with being a woman is to realize that we are naturally loving, responsible, and intelligent people.

> ➤ <u>Learn speaking skills: How to communicate effectively at any occasion</u>

Image Is Everything! How you introduce yourself is your first impression and lasting impression to whomever you're speaking with. This is where your confidence level is revealed. When you approach someone or they approach you, it is customary to shake hands in business environments. A firm handshake says that you're confident and sure of yourself. A weak handshake says that you're not too sure about yourself, unfortunately.

A clear and pleasant but firm voice is well respected. You should practice your introduction before you speak to others. In fact, with any speaking engagements, it is crucial to be well prepared to keep your confidence level on point. So, try speaking in front of a mirror. Your listener(s) should not have to strain to hear what you have to say to them; speak clear and loud without shouting. Can you imagine the President of the US speaking to the citizens with a low voice and you're straining to hear what's being said? Where's the strength and confidence in this leadership role? You, too, should speak as though you're speaking in front of millions because what you have to say is worth listening to. And, please, don't suck your teeth or chew gum while speaking. The best speakers and people who speak well know what they are talking about before they get started.

Some basic rules to remember when introducing yourself to a group are:

1. The host should greet the guests by introducing themselves first, greet the guest, and escort them to their proper place.

2. When introducing someone to a group, always introduce the person being presented last.

3. Remember to introduce everyone else first and yourself last.

4. A leader, a politician, or a role model should be introduced first before anyone else.

5. Unless the event is about you specifically, try not to talk about yourself too much; just give a short-term version.

> <u>Develop correct standing, walking, and sitting postures</u>

You must be aware of your body language at all times, especially around others. It doesn't hurt to be proper all the time so you don't have to be concerned about whether someone is around or not. Also, your body will habitually slump over if you don't sit up properly. Throughout my childhood, I have attended modeling and charm schools and they all have instructed me basically the same way. So, let's get started. Stand up and envision yourself with a hardback cover book on top of your head, shoulders back, pull your stomach in (at all times), and stand tall.

Now, with regard to your walking skills, it should look and feel natural. Make sure your shoes are comfortable and they support your feet because having discomfort all day due to wearing the wrong shoes can kill your spirit. Walking should be smooth flowing with your personal rhythm and style. Take a look at your walking style in a full length mirror or while you're walking in the mall looking through the store windows. Just observe yourself and make sure you are walking with one foot gracefully in front of the other. Your standing posture should reflect grace and comfort with your head held high and shoulders back. When sitting your posture should be to sit straight up and not slouched over the table or leaning on the chair and your legs closed when seated. Try it in front of a mirror to see what needs improvement, if any, and see what others see.

➢ Learn the Dos and Don'ts of proper etiquette skills

It is useful to know proper etiquette skills especially when you're out and about in the community. What is Etiquette?

1. The customs or rules governing behavior regarded as corrector acceptable in social or official life, or

2. Conventional but unwritten code of practice followed by members of any certain profession or group

Clear communication is very important when others determine how they view you. Let's discuss your telephone and speaking etiquette. Your tone as well as the information you speak or convey gives the listener an understanding of who you are and what level of education you have received. A great rule of thumb is to remember that you should speak to others the way you would like to be spoken to in return. Also, make sure you listen to what the speaker is saying before you respond; you might not fully understand what they are saying until they complete their thought. Make sure you're clear with what you want to say and what you want the listener to understand.

When on the telephone, make sure you have a smile on your face; it makes a big difference as far as what the listener is thinking about you and what you have to say, unless you're calling about an unfortunate situation. Even then, if you need to speak regarding a negative circumstance, you must remember to stay calm and communicate effectively. Try to avoid having any noise in your background area; it makes it harder for the listener to hear what you have to say.

Do not have anything in your mouth while speaking: gum, finger, or some other foreign object. It's nothing worse than to see food in someone's mouth while having to look at them as they speak. Do not slurp liquids from a cup or bowl, such as sodas or soups. Slurping gives you gas and that's not lady-like. If you are upset or in a stressful situation, take a deep breath before speaking; remember a Diva is in control of herself at all times. Another thing I need to mention is that I have always been told, and practice it to this day, that when entering into a facility, go straight in. Make your presence known. Seek someone in charge to assist you with where you need to go or what you need to do next.

➢ Develop strategies when dealing with uncomfortable situations and handling them with dignity

There may be a time when you might be in an uncomfortable situation and you need to have a game plan on how to exit the environment. First, always remember that you have class and dignity; therefore, no need to lose control of yourself. In case of an emergency, it is wise to alert someone else IMMEDIATELY! However, if you are in a predicament that you are capable of handling yourself, make yourself clear, look directly at the situation and express whatever needs to be addressed and make your exit – without tripping or slipping on your way out – and they will never forget you and how you handled the situation. People will try to see what you're truly made of.

➤ Learn the benefits of healthy skin care

The main ingredient for healthy skin is water, which is the largest organ of the human body. Keeping your skin properly hydrated will ensure a healthy glow as well. Now, regarding how to create a daily routine for your skin care, there are a few things you need to consider. There is a difference between normal, dry, oily, problem, and combination skin types. Normal skin has a healthy radiance, is elastic, and ages normally. Dry skin has less elasticity, may sometimes burn and tingle, feels tight especially after cleansing, and ages quickly. Oily skin is shiny, is more elastic, and ages slower than the others. Problematic skin is prone to acne, inflamed, very sensitive and requires a lot of cleansing, and ages normally with care. Combination skin usually has a shiny forehead, nose, and chin and the other parts are different giving a T-Shape formation. It usually is elastic, prone to occasional breakouts, and ages normally with care.

I strongly suggest you use this information to research the best products to use for your particular skin and treat it with love because you want to look your best now and when you reach your golden years. It all depends upon how you treat yourself internally and externally. This is another reason why water is so important to your overall well-being.

➤ Apply basic makeup to compliment your beauty – not to prepare you for the circus

Taking into consideration that you are properly caring for your skin, it is safe to apply some basic makeup to compliment your beauty if you are 15 years old or older. If you are in the entertainment industry, in some cases you may be younger than 15 wearing makeup. (*It is really up to parents how they want to raise their child/children until they become adults.*)

When choosing a makeup line and other makeup products, it is wise to do some research on the brands' names and see how long they have been in existence. If it is a well-known brand, check out their testimonies over the internet; there's plenty of blogs to choose from or simply by word of mouth. Someone you may know that has taken great care of their skin and their makeup looks flawless might have a great suggestion for you to use. Not too much is needed to have a great look because the best look is to look like you – unique and flawless! Not painted with tons of colors; unless you are a clown.

Some of the basic products needed to compliment your beauty are:

1. A concealer (applied around the eyes and used to cover blemishes)

2. Foundation (applied over concealer and entire face and neck)

3. Mascara (for eyelashes)

4. Eye shadow

5. Eye pencil

6. Lip pencil

7. Lipstick and/or lip gloss

8. A light blush, if needed

Get a facial at the mall. They're usually free to help encourage you to purchase their products and they are there to answer your makeup questions. Or attend a home party that sells makeup products. Once you have the products, take some time to learn your face and what works well for you. Your makeup is just for you; it's not wise to mix makeup with other people's germs. There is an expiration date applied to some makeup products like foundations and other products; check also to confirm the age of the makeup. The average lifespan of foundation is approximately 3-6 months. Frequently clean the supplies like the brushes you use to apply makeup to your skin. You should change your supplies regularly depending upon the amount of usage. Applying makeup with soiled and dirty supplies may cause infections and breakouts.

➤ Understand basic hair care; choosing shampoos and moisturizers

If you don't have a beautician to consult with, I would like to suggest a few facts. When it comes to choosing a shampoo or moisturizer or whatever is needed for your specific skin type, it's safe to ask someone within your family that has taken care of their body what products they use and why. Another way to determine which shampoo to use is to remember that if you treat your hair; such as, a *perm,* blow dry regularly, or you dye your hair different colors, you should use an acid-balanced shampoo.

Always use a hair conditioner to protect your hair from drying out, and it gives your hair a fresh smell as well. It is best to keep your scalp moisturized especially if you have a dry scalp and dry skin everywhere else. The best moisturizers for your body that I recommend are the natural ones with ingredients such as shea butter, coco butter, aloe or coconut based products. They are great for the skin and in your hair, too. Lotions and potions are also good if you have oily skin or non-dry skin.

➢ <u>Learn proper upkeep for hand and feet care</u>

A Diva must always have soft hands and feet for haters to have something else to talk about you. You know they're searching for something to complain about. When your hands and feet are soft to the touch, it's a sign that you love yourself and you take care of yourself. By the way, they will talk about you if you're good or bad, sad or happy, tall or short, awake or sleepy. My point is to ignore people that have meaningless conversations. It takes away from your natural beauty and you don't need to fill your brain with such nonsense.

Now, when it comes to your hands and feet, you should have a regular manicure and pedicure. If you're on a limited budget or simply like to do it yourself or together with a friend, you should make sure you have the basic products necessary for a well-polished look:

1. Cotton balls

2. Nail polish remover

3. Emery board

4. Nail trimmer

5. Nail polish

6. Cotton gloves.

Clear or a pearl-colored nail polish is the best choice to use for your fingernails. Any color you desire is allowed on your toes, unless you have to go somewhere with your toes exposed and you are in a business environment. During those occasions, it is wise to use a solid soft color, possibly clear.

SELF – ANALYSIS
Assessment

Chapter 2

1. What does being a woman mean to you?

    _____
    _____
    _____
    _____
    _____

2. What makes you different from the male species?

    _____
    _____
    _____
    _____
    _____

3. What will you do if you ever come across an uncomfortable situation? Please explain.

    _____
    _____
    _____
    _____
    _____

4. What will be your general routine for entering into an unfamiliar environment?

    _____
    _____
    _____
    _____
    _____

5. What are the some of the products you use to keep fresh and clean?   Why those products?

_____

_____

_____

_____

_____

6. If you had more confidence, what would you do differently?

_____

_____

_____

_____

_____

7. Do you need makeup to feel better? Explain.

_____

_____

_____

_____

_____

8. What's your skin type? Explain how to care for your specific skin tone.

_____

_____

_____

_____

_____

9. What's the best way to care for your hands and feet?

_____

_____

_____

_____

_____

10. How will your first impression be given? How will you introduce yourself?

_____
_____
_____
_____
_____
_____

11. If you are not aware of who you are yet, how will you explain yourself to others? What are your positive traits and talents and/or skills?

_____
_____
_____
_____
_____
_____

Notes:

Chapter Three:

Knowing Your Self-Worth:

Chapter Summary:
This chapter is designed to teach and encourage you to understand your true value, which is that you come from greatness, no matter what your current circumstances are. Learn to love yourself unconditionally! What's your passion? What's your calling? You will learn to identify the battles within your mind and seek positive solutions. Understand your direction in life. What's your level of esteem? You will have a better understanding that sex does not determine your worth. You are more than your body parts. Most of all, lack of personal worth makes some feel limited in their abilities to obtain what they really want out of life. End unhealthy relationships and have a better understanding of the value of your mind, body, and soul.

> ***Statistics Show: We have the highest rates of teen pregnancy and births which costs at least $10 Billion annually.***

Self-worth (n.) The sense of one's own value or worth as a person; self-esteem; self-respect.

This chapter will help you:

> ➤ Learn the value of unconditional love

Real love cannot be sold. Unconditional love is the highest level of love you can give to someone else. You are saying to them "No matter what, I will always love you." That's a powerful gift to give. Let's make sure they've earned it. You can do this in so many different ways; but first, how do you know if they're worth giving your love to? Firstly, time is a truth factor. Be patient; time tells all. If someone loves you, they know that you're worth the wait. However, if a situation feels uncomfortable, chances are you need to listen to your intuition and think your way through the situation. Don't allow anyone steal your joy.

Unconditional love is like when you have a loyal pet. They love you and there is nothing you can do to make them stop loving you. They still want to play with you if you had a good or bad day, if you gained a little weight, or if you had nothing to offer them but your hugs, that's more than enough for those that want to see you succeed in life. That's unconditional love.

Listen, people are capable of making mistakes. *Have you ever made a mistake?* The rule here is to be you at all times and enjoy life. Of course you will go through awkward situations at time, that's a part of life. It helps you grow, if you learn from those life lessons. If the people around you are not enjoying life, you are better off trying to relocate yourself into a healthier environment. This is why education is extremely important.

➤ Understand the battles of your mind and how to make right choices

You have the power to control your thoughts. Choices need to be well thought out before you act. Dream, don't drift by in life! Inspiration with determination equals success! How you act determines how you think of yourself. Pay attention to your thoughts. Are you thankful for what you have? Have you learned the power of forgiveness? Are you imprisoned in your mind and want to break free? Do you allow others to determine your mood? What do you say to yourself? If you can't change your immediate environment, you can change your mindset and create a goal to change your circumstances more positively in your favor. If you can't change your environment immediately due to situations beyond your control, you can create a plan and work towards your desired results.

There are some very articulate, smart, and beautiful people that can't win the battles within their heads when it comes to chasing things and people that aren't any good for them and their desired peace of mind. How do you love someone unconditionally and still have enough love for yourself? If you can't afford it, don't try to break your bank account, unless it's a necessity for you to survive. Are you happy with your decisions? Is it better to appear to look good to others at the price of hurting emotionally? Do you care about what others think about you or how you feel about yourself? Insist on having healthy relationships with the people you choose to surround yourself with. If you're related to someone by blood or marriage and you don't necessarily get along with them, or it can be an instructor or supervisor or employer, it's wise to try to avoid being in their environment as much as possible. Situations like these could create battles within your mind, but remember to treat others the way you would like to be treated and continue with your goals and in time you'll be fine.

➤ Discover who you truly are and the direction you want to take throughout your lifetime

Throughout your lifetime you want to be prepared along your journey. The way to prepare yourself is to write it down or create a document and/or save it on your laptop in an electronic folder along with your other great ideas to get you ahead in life and hopefully to help our society as well. No matter what direction you take in life, you want to make sure that it fits you and your needs naturally and comfortably. You need to have a healthy understanding of who you are and what your values are.

You have a healthy understanding of your value when:

1. You feel good about yourself during your highs and your lows.

2. You know that you're capable of accomplishing goals.

3. You know that you're not perfect; however, you're the best at being you.

4. You look forward to each new day full of anticipation and a willingness to learn.

5. You know that sex does not determine your worth.

6. Your friendship is valuable and should be handled with care.

7. You don't get all upset if someone doesn't want to befriend you.

8. You have a well thought-out plan for your success.

9. You are expecting your unplanned blessings because you're a giver.

10. You take your life seriously consisting of your mind, body, and soul.

➢ Learn how to make positive choices

Every day we have to make choices. Small choices are whether we want to wear black or blue skirt. Bigger choices would consist of what career or profession you would like to choose for your lifestyle. The choices you decide to choose can have lasting results that follow. If it's a bad choice, negativity follows; if it's a good choice, positivity follows. Try not to make a rush decision, especially if it involves a critical issue in your life. If it's possible, even if you're sure of your choices at the moment, try to sleep on it or give a definite answer within 24 hours. This gives you time to get passed the excitement or terror of the issue and your emotions have calmed and you can think rationally and logically.

➢ Learn the symptoms of suffering from low self-esteem

People who suffer from a lack of self-esteem:

1. Believe that they can't help themselves – they have *bad luck*

2. Believe that things will only get better if they won a large sum of money

3. Believe that their looks or their body parts determine who they are

4. Believe that outside events and relationships determine their happiness

5. Believe that they are different from successful people and can't catch up

People suffer unknowingly from having a low self-esteem. When you have a low self-esteem it means that you do not yet know the true value you behold. Spiritually speaking, each and every one of us is special and unique. Embrace who you are and understand that no one is perfect. Those kind of thoughts of feeling upset and depressed because life is not exactly what you thought it would be or whatever the case is, you must stop the negative thinking immediately and remember that the task at hand for you is to discover who you truly are and maximize your opportunities.

You should realize that inwardly you are a complete being. It's the outer circumstances, situations, and events that may make you feel confused about who you are. Then you start to believe that those events directly affect who you are as a person. Situations and events are not you. Our Creator has given you a soul that was never born and will never die. You are more than your body. You are more than your mind. These are tools used to aide and help you function together properly for your soul. Therefore, be mindful of what you put into your mind (garbage, useless conversations, and time killing situations) and be mindful of what you put into your body (junk food, all kinds of man-made chemicals and artificial additives and products) and stick to the basics: greens, beans, wheat, vegetables, and plenty of water. Your body will thank you now and you will thank yourself later when you see others that didn't take advantage of having a healthy life routine. All of this needs to be balanced in order to live a *Divalicious* lifestyle!

➤ Discover your calling through your passions

What do you enjoy most in life? Let's say, for example, if you did not have to pay any bills and had all the time in the world to do anything, what would it be? Now, it's up to you to decide how to capitalize on your passion. Another example is that you could love to help others. If that is the case, I suggest finding a profession around assisting others and receiving income for your help. I discuss branding later on for those interested in starting your own business. There is no magic age you have to be in order to start your own business. All it takes is passion, determination, and skill to achieve your goals.

➤ Learn the value of your physical body, mind, and soul

Try to imagine that your body is like a vehicle used to help you function on the planet for your soul. Your body needs proper fuel/food to give you the best results. Exercise is vitally important to ensure that you are keeping your body in top notch condition and can handle any physical situation should you need to walk or excessively move your body around for an extended period of time without wearing your body down.

Your mind is your mechanism for functioning on this planet as well. You can fill it up with the necessary information to maximize your opportunities in life or you can fill it full of garbage and unnecessary information that's totally useless for securing your financial future and a life full of drama. I'm sure you know the best choices to make when it comes to taking care of you, your mind, and having peace of mind.

I saved the best for last. The soul, the essence of you; which cannot respond to the senses; you can't touch your soul, smell your soul, taste your soul, etc. However, it's the soul that directs the mind and body. What do you like to do most? What's your passion? These are the things that let you know just how unique and special you are because no one else has the same exact anything alike; not even identical twins.

➢ <u>Learn positive affirmations to omit negativity</u>

Negative thoughts will come to mind and you have to have the strength to know when it's taking over your thoughts and you must make the decision to stop the madness immediately. Start observing each situation carefully and start thinking about what is actually taking place and how to change the circumstances for the better.

Positive Affirmations:

1. I love myself unconditionally.

2. I have a purpose in life and I will pursue it.

3. I will joyously assist others who will appreciate my assistance.

4. I can accomplish anything I put my mind to.

5. I am truly thankful for all that I have and all of the unexpected blessings that are to come.

What's Your Worth?

Self-worth (n.) of one's own value or worth as a person; self-esteem; self-respect.

Your self-worth comes in handy when you want to increase your self-esteem because you need to be able to observe yourself and your actions and see if there are any flaws that you have and you know you're capable of doing better, it's just a matter of removing bad habits and replacing them with positive habits.

Where is your level of self-worth? The questions following are for you to really give honest answers only to prepare you for your best outcome. No matter what you have experienced either really exciting or really traumatic, you must maintain control of yourself at all times. We all have had situations that we will always cherish as well as situations that we remember from the past that may not have put us in good situations; however, we get through it. That's when you learn to let go of the past pain and always remember that tomorrow is another day and another chance to make a difference in this world.

Now, the best way to answer these questions is to write your first thought that comes to mind because this is how you're able to see who you are at this moment in time. Your answer to each question should correlate with this score scale:

1- Disagree strongly
2- Disagree somewhat
3- Can't make up my mind
4- Agree somewhat
5- Agree strongly

• I don't let others' opinions of me (good or bad) distract me from my goals.   5 4 3 2 1

• Situations that are unexpected come, but it can't stop my progress.   5 4 3 2 1

• Even though I might temporally get distracted, I will still complete the task.   5 4 3 2 1

• If no one else likes me, I will be okay.   5 4 3 2 1

• I can remain in control of myself at all times.   5 4 3 2 1

• I know if I put myself up to the challenge, I will succeed.   5 4 3 2 1

• If someone that I like doesn't like me, I'm okay with that. It's their loss.   5 4 3 2 1

• I know I'm the only one truly holding me back. I can do better.   5 4 3 2 1

• If my plans didn't work out, I will just start preparing a better plan.   5 4 3 2 1

• I know I need to eat the best in order to feel the best.   5 4 3 2 1

• I have time on my side to get to know my true friends.   5 4 3 2 1

As soon as you complete this questionnaire, tally your results and evaluate your score:

If you have a score between 41 – 50, that means that you have a high self-esteem and this is good because you need to have a high self-esteem and confidence level in order to succeed in life and obtain the lifestyle you want to have and maintain it. You Rock!

If you have a score between 31 and 40 that means you can get by in life without too much chaos; however, you need to improve on your image of you. There will be times in which you might not have the best answer or know exactly what to do and with a little practice, you'll do fine. No one is born with self-esteem but you can improve it daily. Setting goals and accomplish them is one way of improving how you feel about yourself. But also, you can't allow others to tell you how you feel. You know you better than anyone else.

If you have a score between 21 and 30 that means you're not really sure of who you are and why you're here or what your purpose in life really is. No one is perfect, but you should like yourself and if you don't or you're just not sure what's going on, remember that if you put your focus on our Creator and pray for answers while willing to receive what's needed, you will be given all that you desire.

If you have a score between 10 and 20 that means that prayer should be first in your life, if you want to obtain the correct answers quickly and efficiently. This is a sign of low self-esteem and if this is the case, you need to analyze your thinking pattern and why you don't believe in yourself. I would strongly suggest talking with a loved one or an instructor/advisor if you're in a really bad rut and you can't shake it off. That's what instructors/advisors are there for. There are solutions to your problems. You can succeed in life. You can create your destiny! You can do it!

SELF – ANALYSIS
Assessment

Chapter 3

1. Who are some of the people that you have unconditional love for?

_____
_____
_____
_____
_____

2. Explain some of the battles of your mind and how you plan to make right choices.

_____
_____
_____
_____
_____

3. Have you discovered someone you thought was your friend and they really weren't? Explain how you found out and what you did, if anything.

_____
_____
_____
_____
_____

4. How do you make positive choices when it comes to your deepest temptations?

_____
_____
_____
_____
_____

5. Are you suffering from low self-esteem? Why or Why Not?

_____
_____
_____
_____
_____

6. List some of your passions.

_____
_____
_____
_____
_____

7. What are some of the ways your body has value?

_____
_____
_____
_____
_____

8. What are some of the ways your mind has value?

_____
_____
_____
_____
_____

9. What are some of the ways your soul has value?

_____
_____
_____
_____
_____

10. What other positive things can you do for yourself to appreciate who you are?

_____
_____
_____
_____
_____

Notes:

Chapter Four:

There's an Art to Being Smart:

Chapter Summary:
This chapter is designed to help demonstrate the infinite variety of resources available for gaining knowledge. It teaches the importance of investing in oneself with education, preparing for the future and having fun in the process! You will learn the "hard" truths about how expensive it is to be ignorant in life and in business. You will also be prepared to make sound decisions to ensure you lead a productive, successful, fulfilling life! **Example:** *How will you be able to set goals and afford to maintain your lifestyle independently as an adult?*

Statistics Show: Some girls believe it's cute to appear dumb.

Smart: (adj.) Astute, as in business; clever or bright. 2. Quick, witty

This chapter will help you:

➢ Decide your chosen profession

The internet is a great tool for gathering information. The library as well and they have a staff ready to assist you should you need assistance during your research. Information is very available and valuable; and ignorance is very expensive. The more you know, the less amount of money will be spent on correcting errors that could have been possibly prevented. Different careers can be explored to help you discover who you are and what you like doing best. School is pivotal when choosing a career or profession that will support you financially for years.

The 15 top paying careers: *(CNBC 2012)*

- **15. Pharmacist**
  Average Salary: $112,160

- **14. Air Traffic Controller**
  Average annual salary: $114,460

- **13. Sales Managers**
  Average annual salary: $116,860

- **12. Airline Pilots, Copilots and Flight Engineers**
  Average annual salary: $118,070

- **11. Financial Manager**
  Average annual salary: $120,450

- **10. Industrial-Organizational Psychologists**
  Average annual salary: $124,160

- **9. Computer and Information Systems Managers**
  Average annual salary: $125,660

- **8. Marketing Managers**
  Average annual salary: $126,190

- **7. Natural Science Managers**
  Average annual salary: $128,230

- **6. Architectural and Engineering Managers**
  Average annual salary: $129,350

- **5. Lawyer**
  Average annual salary: $130,490

- **4. Petroleum Engineer**
  Average annual salary: $138,980

- **3. Chief Executive Officers**
  Average annual salary: $176,550

- **2. Orthodontists and Dentists**
  Average annual salary: $161,750-$204,670

- **1. Doctors and Surgeons**
  Average annual salary: $168,650-$234,950

The amount of money should not be the main reason you choose a career. If, however, you have skills or interests similar to top paying careers like the ones listed above, they can be great choices for you to consider. No matter what career you choose, take the time to make sure it's a great fit for you and your passion in life. If you want nothing more than to become the best mother and housewife that's fine just be the best you can be. Your choices in life should complement who you are.

➤ Develop skills to prepare for success

Challenge your passion. Don't let anything deter you from accomplishing your goals. You create your destiny by simply believing in yourself first and staying focused and diligent all along the way.

Skills needed for success are:

- Discipline
- Time Management skills
- Problem-Solving skills
- A willingness to listen and learn
- Responsible
- Respectful towards others
- Confidence
- A desire to win at all cost

➤ Learn how to have fun while you're learning

Learning is a never-ending process. Therefore, enjoy your journey while learning. Acquiring new facts is great because it prepares you for whatever your direction is in life. That's the key to success! We have to survive because we exist. You can choose to enjoy your journey or choose to live life without purpose and hope for the best. Life is full of possibilities and disappointments and the more prepared you are for success the chances are that you will receive what you put your mind to. What you think most about should be what your goals are in life.

➤ Understand your lifestyle's comfort zone and what's needed to acquire it

Where do you want to be in five years? Now is the time to prepare for that time and space. Where do you want to live? How do you want to travel? What will you eat? All of this adds up once you create a chart explaining what exactly you want out of life in order to help you understand what kind of revenue is needed to acquire that particular lifestyle. It's simply creating a map and following it unless some changes need to be made along the way to improve your plans. Take timeout to get to know you better.

➤ Ignorance of the law is no excuse – do your research

A Diva not only looks good on the inside and outside but also has a classy demeanor about her. You can't look classy and classless at the same time. Know what you're talking about or simply state the fact that you cannot comment because you are not familiar with the topic and will get back to them. Read! Always try to read something every day. Inspirational material is good and also be aware of what's going on in and around the world. If you can, it's a good idea to learn the basic law of the land. It's very useful to protect you from scams and to learn how to stay legal. Did you know in some states it's still against the law to cross in the middle the street but so many people do it every day? You don't want to be the person they decide to practice that law on.

➢ <u>Learn how to set goals</u>

One great tool I use to set goals is to write it down on paper. Writing down your thoughts not only helps you see your thoughts clearly, but it also helps you plan out your thoughts and you can always go back and adjust your plans while following your personal map towards success.

Directions for accomplishing your specific goal(s):

1. Write out the specific goal. It's better to accomplish one at a time, if possible.

2. List the tasks needed in order to obtain the goal.

3. Begin working on the tasks. Write your thoughts. Add to the tasks, when and if needed.

4. Check off the tasks as they are completed.

5. When all of the tasks are completed, determine if the goal has been met. If so, begin working on your next goal. If your goal has not been met, decide what needs improvement, revise your goal, and begin again with the new tasks.

6. Create a new sheet/outline and start again at number one.

➢ <u>Understand the purpose of a budget</u>

The purpose of a budget is to help you have peace of mind. Even if you have millions of dollars, it's wise to use a budget to know where your money is coming and going. Pennies add up. If you spend a little here and a little there, after a while, it's gone. Make your own specific budget and know the amounts associated with each category.

What to list when creating a budget:

- Income and taxes withheld
- Expenses at home – bills, self-care, etc.
- Food
- Transportation
- Recreation/Entertainment
- Savings
- Emergency funds

➤ Learn how to live a productive life

Ah, to live a productive life is to appreciate every moment through the good and the bad. If you create an environment in which you can be productive and enjoy what you do, it won't seem like work. The more well planned your life is and you stay focused, you know where you're going in life and you can see your accomplishments and desires fulfilled.

➤ Learn how to stay on target

You will always be tempted to do something else that will get you off of your target project. Therefore, it is important to learn how to firmly say no if someone asks you to do something that will take you way off of your focus and is totally meaningless. Don't get me wrong, there's a time to work and then there's time to play even harder. But you want to be able to celebrate a conquest not just partying just to party; after a while it becomes worthless. You can have so much more fun if you choose your time wisely.

➤ Understand the importance of inspiration, motivation, and dedication

From time to time everyone needs encouragement. It's great to be able to depend on you for your own inspiration. Hopefully, you want to succeed in life in order to have peace of mind depending upon your personal financial security. Take some personal time with yourself to process your thoughts without distractions and then you can share your love and time with others because they're a part of you. Throughout the day think about your goals and what will be the result of you sticking to your dedication for success.

SELF – ANALYSIS
Assessment

Chapter 4

1. What are some of the resources available for gaining knowledge?

   _____
   _____
   _____
   _____
   _____

2. What skills/goals are needed to prepare you for your future success?

   _____
   _____
   _____
   _____
   _____

3. Explain how you can have fun while you're learning.

   _____
   _____
   _____
   _____
   _____

4. What are some of your lifestyle's comfort zone and what's needed to acquire it?

   _____
   _____
   _____
   _____
   _____

5. What research is necessary for you to achieve your goals?

_____
_____
_____
_____
_____

6. What's the best way for you to achieve your goals?

_____
_____
_____
_____
_____

7. What do you understand regarding the purpose of a following a budget?

_____
_____
_____
_____
_____

8. How will you apply what you have learned for living a productive life?

_____
_____
_____
_____
_____

9. What are the ways you stay focused in order to accomplish your goals?

_____
_____
_____
_____
_____

10. Do you have quotes you use for inspiration, motivation, and dedication?

_____

_____

_____

_____

_____

Notes:

Chapter Five:

You Must Get Fit:

Chapter Summary:
This chapter is designed to cover topics that are important for maintaining what is considered to be a healthy physical lifestyle. How do you look in the mirror - completely nude? Healthy lifestyles consist of eating, sleeping, and exercising properly on a regular routine, which will help create environments that encourage your body and brain to work at its maximum effort. Learn how to combat your fears and defeat procrastination with good habits.

Statistics Show: Girls most dissatisfied with their body shape become depressed.

Exercise: (v.) bodily or mental exertion, especially for training or improvement of health

This chapter will help you:

➢ Learn how to eat

Having had children, I gained a few pounds and found it difficult to get back to my normal size. Until I learned about the relationship I have with food, I don't think I would have ever lost the weight. I lost over 50 pounds and I look and feel great! I love food, but I don't want it to kill me. Therefore, I had to learn about the importance of eating healthy because just exercising was not enough to get the unwanted fat off of my body.

For the average person, if you don't work off the calories that you consume throughout the day, it has no choice but to stick to your belly, legs, and arms. Stop the madness! Food is to be consumed to give the body energy to handle your day-to-day activities. Food was not created solely to please your taste buds. If you are addicted to food there's professional help for you to learn how to eat properly. Don't let food control you. A change of habit(s) could be all that's needed to learn to eat healthier.

Eating has to do with timing and portion control. My family eats something every three to four hours a day while we're burning energy throughout the day. We eat the biggest meal when we know we will burn the most energy. The portion control is also important because if you eat more than you can burn, it will stick around – around your belly, legs, and arms. Eat healthy food responsibly.

➢ Learn how to drink - proper fluid intake

If you look at the examples all around us, you will notice that this planet is made mainly of water. Everywhere you turn people discuss the importance for a healthy supply of water intake daily. Therefore, if you drink sugar drinks, try to drink 3 glasses of water to every glass of liquid sugar-product. Here's some useful information from mangosteen-natural-remedies.com:

"The human body is anywhere from 55% to 78% water depending on body size. A rule of thumb, 2/3 of body is consists of water, and it is the main component of human body. Did you know that your tissues and organs are mainly made up of water? Here is the %:

- Muscle consists of 75% water
- Brain consists of 90% of water
- Bone consists of 22% of water
- Blood consists of 83% water

The functions of water in human body are vital. The water:

- Transports nutrients and oxygen into cells
- Moisturizes the air in lungs
- Helps with metabolism
- Protects our vital organs
- Helps our organs to absorb nutrients better
- Regulates body temperature
- Detoxifies
- Protects and moisturizes our joints

Every cell in your body needs water from head to toe. That is why it is so important to drink enough fluid. Take for example, brain consists of 90% of water, if you do not supply enough water to your body, your brain cannot function well, and you will get headache or migraine. Hence, next time, if you feel fatigue and headache, it may be the sign of dehydration."

➢ Understand what a healthy physical lifestyle consists of

Your life should be well balanced in order for you to feel complete. Don't try to fake it, what good does it serve? People know you're not telling the truth anyway. So, they pretend to pretend with you. Life is meant to be enjoyed to the fullest and that means not having to cage your peace of mind and feeling free. Spread your wings and discover all that life has to give you. Life is not just here for you to be born and learn how to walk, talk, work, party, retire and that's the end of the line. No, you must discover what you're specifically here to do and you know you're on point if it involves helping move the world and mankind forward. Then, once you know why you're here and you're achieving your goals and taking care of yourself mentally, physically and spiritually, you will be living a healthy physical lifestyle.

You can look at yourself in the mirror naked and like what you see. Your body can look and feel better by building muscles and getting a firmer figure; you also experience other benefits as well. Muscle for example, burns more calories while you are resting. This helps contribute to weight loss. Exercise and physical activity also reduce the risk of premature death, improve psychological well-being, and reduce the risk of developing and/or dying from heart disease.

➢ Set regular exercise goals

Exercise is not a fad or a quick diet trick. It's a lifestyle. You should have a weekly scheduled time solid on your calendar when you work out. It's best to work out at least 3-4 times a week, resting in between days. My husband, Sir Markadoo, who is a fitness trainer would say, "It establishes a routine and gets you prepared to develop your own body. That's the biggest self-expression anyone can establish. This prepares you for everything else you do in life. Setting goals and making your mind prepared for greatness."

Tips for consistent exercise:

- Schedule some exercise time every day, even if it's just a few minutes.

- Split up your workouts. You can get the same benefit from short workouts spread throughout the day along with continuous workouts. Just move your body.

- Change daily routines to give yourself more time to walk, run, or dance. Also, you want to keep it challenging and fun.

- Make exercise your focus and schedule the rest of your day around it instead of trying to fit exercise into your busy day. It's a lifestyle commitment.

➢ How to combat the fears in the mind

We must go through mental battles in order to grow. Hopefully, we grow and never need to repeat that lesson again in life. A great technique is to have time to yourself every morning before you start your day. All it takes is a few minutes of sitting in a comfortable chair and thinking through the thoughts that take time to figure out the best solution to the situations. The answers might not come right away, but if you try this technique every day, it gets easier and easier to come to the best solutions to your problems all the time. Try not to go around town telling everyone your situations, especially if they are not familiar with giving proper and professional assistance.

➢ Learn how to resist unhealthy foods and drinks

Everything takes practice to get better at whatever it is you want to improve upon. Unhealthy foods are those that smell and taste the best! However, everything you see is not good for you and you must stay balanced. Eating healthy most of the time is much better than not eating healthy at all. I'm an 80/20. I eat healthy 80% of the time. I like to eat snacks from time to time; however, if I eat something full of calories, I make sure I burn it off before the night is over with exercise.

➢ Analyze your habits

How are your habits? What do you think about most? Start there. What you think about most is of most value to you at this moment. Sit back and analyze why you choose to think about what you think about out of all the things you could be thinking about, why? If you have been a victim of an unfortunate situation understand that's the past and you deserve much better. If you're not able to overcome a horrific situation, please seek professional help. Seek the answers from a reliable source. Once you get over your past, you can move onto your exciting new future! If you're just plain lazy, try to realize that your time is being eaten up by trying to find things that if you simply had a special spot for each item to begin with you can save so much time and less headaches.

➢ Stop procrastinating and get up

The only thing stopping you from success is your efforts. Some of the things you want to achieve might not necessarily be easy to obtain, but if it's been done before, chances are you can do it too!

Tips to help prevent procrastination:

- Make realistic goals to complete tasks

- Break the project up into steps and work on each one separately

- Create a timeline for each step – put it on a calendar

- Reward yourself when you complete steps

- Associate with like-minded responsible people

- Seek helpful information to broaden your horizon and inspire you to change any bad habits

➢ Learn the importance of proper rest on a daily basis

If you don't receive the proper amount of rest every 24 hours, you will not be a happy camper. You might not even notice it but unless you receive 6-8 hours (at least) you will more than likely not be at your best performance throughout the time you're awake. That's not fair to you.

Insufficient sleep dulls awareness, causes mental confusion, contributes to emotional instability, impairs concentration, and weakens the body's immune system. Get your proper rest. You have the power to create an environment of honor and respect. Nowadays, we live to see 90 years of age and beyond. You want to preserve your Diva*ness* as long as possible. Sleep is a very important ingredient to the recipe for the fountain of life. According to Emedicinehealth.com:

In humans, it has been demonstrated that the metabolic activity of the brain decreases significantly after 24 hours of sustained wakefulness. Sleep deprivation results in a decrease in body temperature, a decrease in immune system function as measured by white blood cell count (the soldiers of the body), and a decrease in the release of growth hormone. Sleep deprivation can also cause increased heart rate variability.
For our nervous systems to work properly, sleep is needed. Sleep deprivation makes a person drowsy and unable to concentrate the next day. It also leads to impairment of memory and physical performance and reduced ability to carry out mathematical calculations. If sleep deprivation continues, hallucinations and mood swings may develop."

SELF – ANALYSIS
Assessment

Chapter 5

1. What's your regular routine for eating every day?

   _____
   _____
   _____
   _____
   _____

2. What's your proper daily water intake? What other fluids do you drink regularly?
   What purpose do they serve?

   _____
   _____
   _____
   _____
   _____

3. What do you consider to be a healthy lifestyle for you to follow?

   _____
   _____
   _____
   _____
   _____

4. Do you like to exercise? What's your idea of a healthy workout regimen for you to
   follow?

   _____
   _____
   _____
   _____
   _____

5. What will be the difference between your regular workout and your rigorous workout?

_____
_____
_____
_____
_____

6. How do you combat the fears within your mind?

_____
_____
_____
_____
_____

7. What are some of the ways you resist unhealthy foods and drinks?

_____
_____
_____
_____
_____

8. What are some habits that you are having trouble with the most? Explain.

_____
_____
_____
_____
_____

9. What do you think about most? Is it harmful or helpful? Please Explain.

_____
_____
_____
_____
_____

10. Identify the things you don't like to do, which makes you want to procrastinate. How will you improve accomplishing uneasy tasks?

_____
_____
_____
_____
_____
_____

11. What are your regular (or not regular) sleeping habits? How can it improve?

_____
_____
_____
_____
_____
_____

Notes:

Chapter Six:

Mastering Self-Control:

Chapter Summary:
This chapter is designed to cover topics such as mastering your emotions. You will learn stress-reduction tips for everyday stressors and traumatic situations as well. You will learn how to take a personal timeout before they start the day and the importance of breathing. You will develop ways to avoid bullies and their games. Understand how to defeat self-doubt with the power of your words. Learn how to love yourself. Also, learn how to handle "Haters" and have peace of mind, all the time. Get to know yourself on a more personal note. You are unique!

Statistics Show: Arrests of girls for violent offenses continue to rise in the America.

Self-Control: (n.) Control or restraint of oneself or one's actions, feelings, etc.

This chapter will help you:

➢ <u>Learn how to control your emotions</u>

Power is useless without control. The best way to enjoy life is to have control of your thoughts and emotions. Breathing is a great technique to gain immediate access to controlling yourself if you feel you are losing it. Learn how to count to ten, it works.

➢ <u>Learn how to see the warning signs of danger</u>

Warning signs of danger can be all around if you take notice of the situation you're faced with that involves some trouble. You have an intuition that tells you that something is not right and you need to take flight and exit as soon as possible. It might not be a situation that you can immediately escape; it might be in your household and you're not able to leave right away. What do you do? That's when you have to intelligently and not emotionally come up with a solution that will uplift you and your image in the long run. If there is trouble somewhere close like within the household, calmly discuss it with your parents. Communicating effectively is the best way to ensure healthy relationships. If your attempts fail with attempting to communicating effectively with your parents, then request professional assistance for the entire family in order to learn how to come together in a lovingly manner.

➢ <u>Understanding what triggers your emotions</u>

Everyone has something they like and dislike. We are all unique and come from different backgrounds and environments. Some people's environments were pleasant and for others they may have grown up in unpleasant environments. No matter where we come from, we all have learning lessons along the way. It's important to recognize your level of comfort and understand what triggers your emotions. Don't let people get you so mad that you can't think straight; you will be giving them the power to control you.

➢ <u>Develop ways to avoid bullies and their games</u>

Bully: (n.) A blustering, quarrelsome, overbearing person who habitually badgers and intimidates smaller or weaker people.

Bullies come in all shapes and sizes and ages. They don't care about you at all! They are unhappy and want everyone within their path to experience their unhappiness. They tend to gravitate towards people that they feel they can easily hurt, see a hurtful response, and think they're able to get away with it. There are different ways people can become victims of a bully or group bulling:

- Name calling
- Rude gestures
- Gossiping
- Social exclusion
- Fighting
- Pretending to be someone's friend to set them up later
- Intimidation
- Destroying property
- Shouting to embarrass
- Witness(es) – person or group not doing anything about what's observed

The important thing to remember is that if someone approaches you and throughout the conversation you begin to realize that they don't care about you and want to push a negative energy your way, you must realize that you don't have to accept what someone else wants to give you because they think they are taller, smarter, older, cuter, stronger, richer, more talented, or whatever the case is. You are much more valuable than that. You do not have to be afraid of threats and powerless words. I used the word powerless because only you can give their threats and words power. Bullies think about who they want to attack before the victim sees it coming. Therefore, protect yourself at all times by using your brain and understanding that you may not see it coming, but once it's there, use your intelligence to get yourself out of that situation in order to handle it correctly and professionally at a later time; once you're clear from danger.

If you believe your life is in danger, seek the authorities immediately. If you believe your life is not in danger but you have someone or some people who want to make your life difficult, remember that after you pray for guidance, make sure you protect yourself from immediate danger by getting away from the situation. Now, that doesn't mean that you're afraid of the person, it simply means that you're smart enough to know that you don't need to be around negative people and negative environments to prove you're right.

There have been times where bullies will have a weapon or an object and really wants to cause bodily harm to you if you don't do what they want you to do. Every situation is different, but if you can avoid getting hurt and seeking a secured location, that's the best solution. It's a good idea to learn how to protect yourself with a self-defense course.

➤ Unveil the power you have within you

With our uniqueness we are able to maximize our potential by mastering our special gift. I enjoy assisting others and observing positive growth through setting and achieving goals. When I learned how to adjust my negative thoughts by simply not giving the thoughts any time to corrupt my mind, I noticed that I had the power to eliminate whatever is not healthy for me because I'm better than that!

➤ Learn to ignore ignorance

Every day you are faced with studying, working, or just trying to relax and someone wants to steal your time with their ignorance and ignorant behavior. Your time is valuable and you should love yourself enough to know that you don't have time to listen to garbage and filter all of that mess through your precious brain. Why? Life has so much to offer, why waste it on garbage.

➤ Learn to like yourself first

You should be excited to learn that if you have at least two true friends that have been there for you in the past and will be there for you through thick and thin and want to see prosper and vice versa, you're at the top of the BFF list because it's rare to have true friends that will not gossip when it's convenient for them about you. When you love yourself, a situation like this won't aggravate you. What difference does it make if everyone in the room doesn't find you attractive or want to spend their time with you. It's okay to enjoy time with yourself so you can appreciate the great friendship of others.

➤ Defeat self-doubt

No one alive is without some sort of issue or problem they are experiencing, or have experienced in the past, or will experience in the future. Hopefully, you can have the best outcome from each negative experience you go through in life. Nevertheless, we never know when something may happen and we might not believe that we are prepared to handle the situation. You will have times in which you will feel like you doubt yourself. That's when you have to rely on the power of our Creator to pull you through. You have to do your best in order to receive the best outcome throughout all of your situations in life good or bad. The main thing to remember is to understand that when you're faced with doubt about your abilities to get through a situation, you can and you will just like everyone else. That's where the power of faith is required.

➤ Discover what makes you unique

You can learn what makes you unique by observing what you like versus what you definitely don't like. Now, concentrate on what you like to do because this direction will bring you the highest euphoria once you realize what it is that is so special about you.

➢ <u>Learn how to "deal" or "not deal" with *Haters*</u>

"*Haters*" – you can't live with them and you can't live without them because they're all around you.   Haters are not that much different from bullies. And don't let your haters stop you from your accomplishing your goals.   Use them as a tool to sharpen your abilities to conquer evil!!   Seriously, people with self-doubt that refuse to look at themselves and try to make themselves better rather hate on someone who enjoys life and is enjoying their journey.   What do you do with them?   How do you handle these situations?

Well, if you don't have someone hating on you, you haven't arrived either.   Believe me, that's one of the confirmations from your walk in life to success.   If no one has anything to say about you, either good or bad, no one knows of you and that means that you haven't blossomed into the full *you* yet.   If that's the case, what are you waiting for? Dare to shine!   You deserve it!

SELF – ANALYSIS
Assessment

Chapter 6

1. What are some of the ways you control your emotions?

   _____
   _____
   _____
   _____
   _____

2. Have you ever experienced a situation that you saw the signs and were able to save yourself from a lot of trouble? Explain. If not, what do you do to keep from harm?

   _____
   _____
   _____
   _____
   _____

3. Do you ever notice when you're about to blow your top before it happens? What are some of the signals that lets you know that something is about to trigger an unpleasant mood?

   _____
   _____
   _____
   _____
   _____

4. How well do treat yourself and others?

   _____
   _____
   _____
   _____
   _____

5. What are some of the ways to discard your negative traits?

_____
_____
_____
_____
_____

6. What are the unique powers that you possess? How will you unleash your talents?

_____
_____
_____
_____
_____

7. What challenges do you face when having to deal with difficult people?

_____
_____
_____
_____
_____

8. What do you love about you the most? Explain the reasons why.

_____
_____
_____
_____
_____

9. What is currently bothering you and what will you do to end the negativity?

_____
_____
_____
_____
_____

10. Identify the issues, if any, which make you doubt yourself.

_____
_____
_____
_____
_____

_11._ How do you deal, or not deal, with _Haters?_

_____
_____
_____
_____
_____

Notes:

Chapter Seven:

Accepting Responsibility:

Chapter Summary:
This chapter is designed to introduce you to the concept of accepting responsibility. You will understand what skills, resources, and knowledge are needed to accomplish your goals and how to stay focused. Tips for handling stress and peer pressure will also be discussed. **Example: *Do you blame others for your lack of happiness? What obstacles are in the way of you achieving your goals?***
> *Statistics Show: The <u>average</u> person would rather procrastinate than to be responsible.*

Responsibility: (n.) The state or fact of being responsible.

This chapter will help you:

> ➤ <u>The art of accepting responsibility</u>

Accepting responsibility means maturing emotionally. Are you thankful for the opportunities that you have been blessed with thus far? Do you appreciate the people that have helped you along the way? Can you recognize your blessings? The more we mature, the more we accept responsibility and understand the value it brings to our overall character and society as a whole. Being responsible means cheerfully accepting and completing the task at hand. It does you no good to become negative during the process; that's immature.

> ➤ <u>Accept your non-perfect imperfections</u>

Love the skin you're in. Why not? You should love yourself because you know you can depend on yourself when you really want to. You have all the ingredients of a *She-ro* since you've entered into this world. What is perfection? Who is perfect? Being unique people we have various skills that vary from person to person. Discover what makes you shine and accept that you aren't perfect and no one can do you better than you.

> ➤ <u>Tips on how to handle the stress</u>

While at school, make sure your focus is to understand exactly what the instructor wants you to accomplish. If you have any questions, they should be more than happy to assist especially when you show a genuine interest in the subject. Take advantage of the opportunity to learn skills to prepare you for future events and possibly your successful profession. Stress may arise from time to time because you want to focus on school but life gets in the way and it seems as though you're losing hours or you may want to relax but you can't because you've waited until the last minute to handle your responsibilities. No matter what the situation is, you can overcome stress with some simple planning.

Even at home you may feel from time to time that stress is taking over and you feel out of control. The best solution for any situation is to remember to breathe. You have the power of breath and thought. The more prepared you are in any circumstance can ease a stressful or pleasant situation.

➤ Tips on how to handle peer pressure

People will try to see what you're made of, it's natural. Some people may be more persistent than you would prefer them to be and that can be considered peer pressure. And there are some that will try to harm you either emotionally or physically and that can be considered bullying. If someone makes you do something that's not right and you're not comfortable doing it, that's a situation you need to separate yourself from. Seek advice from the counselors at your school, your job, or a trusted family member first before you seek the authorities. The establishment might be able to assist you. You have the right to move freely physically and mentally throughout your school, job, or household.

➤ Learn how to use self-constraint, when necessary

I have been in a few situations where I had to call upon all of my energy to keep me still when I wanted to jump out of my skin! So, if you're ever in a situation where you feel that you want to lose control but you know that later on it's not the best way to handle what happened, always remember to breathe and pray and within a few seconds or minutes, you'll feel so much better. Then, you will be able to think wisely and seek the best solution. Emotions can come on very strong at times without you being prepared for it; therefore, it's good to have this stress-reduction tip to keep you cool at all times.

➤ Learn to laugh out loud

Who's your favorite comedian? I have quite a few of them that I enjoy listening to and some just make you forget where you are and you're just all over the floor trying to catch your breath from laughing so hard! There's nothing better in life than to enjoy a great laugh! Laughing out loud means to enjoy each and every moment because nothing is promised to anyone; therefore, enjoy this experience to the fullest! This includes living a balanced life with handling responsibility, too. Work hard and then play even harder!

➤ Learn stress-reduction techniques

Breathe! That's it. A full breath is what's needed to immediately calm the situation down as far as your mentality is concerned. There will always be situations within your life that you can't control and you may believe you're right and still can't do anything about it; you still must maintain a calm level of thinking. The next tip is to have some time to yourself and just get away from the situation, if possible. Now the wonderful part of these tips is that you don't have to wait until negativity comes your way to appreciate the benefits of breathing properly to lengthen your life.

➢ <u>How to be the "trusted person" in your clique</u>

Until you have fans and hype people around following you everywhere to tell everyone who you are, your reputation is all you have. Don't tarnish it! You never want to hurt someone purposefully; that's a sign that you're unhappy. The best part of life is to enjoy every part of it and when you can hold your head up high at all times, it's a sign of high self-esteem. People yearn for a high self-esteem but don't know how to achieve it. Trust is a valuable tool and you guard your reputation from negativity.

SELF – ANALYSIS
Assessment

Chapter 7

1. How do you accept responsibility when you feel otherwise?

   _____
   _____
   _____
   _____
   _____

2. What are some of the things that are not "perfect" about you but you love anyway?

   _____
   _____
   _____
   _____
   _____

3. Do you get irritated at home , school, or at work? Explain how you can change your situation.

   _____
   _____
   _____
   _____
   _____

4. What are some of the ways your wind down at home and relax?

   _____
   _____
   _____
   _____

5. What are some of the ways you get over anger or disappointment?

_____

_____

_____

_____

_____

6. What are some of the ways you can avoid peer pressure?

_____

_____

_____

_____

_____

7. What can stop you from accomplishing your goals?

_____

_____

_____

_____

_____

Notes:

Chapter Eight:

The Dangers of Mind Altering Substances:

Chapter Summary:
This chapter is designed to teach you the dangers of drugs and the consequences for not accepting self-control. You will be given tips on how to "flee from temptation" and to use discipline when dealing with mind-altering substances. You will learn how to rise above the temptation and make the best choices. You will have the skills to go out and independently make immediate improvements to your life by enjoying life, building wealth, and encouraging others.

Statistics Show: The National Survey on drug use and health indicates 1.5 million girls ages 12-17 started drinking alcohol before legal age.

Additional Statistics Show
According to the NIDA's Monitoring the Future Survey in 2010:

"Measures of <u>marijuana</u> use increased among 8th graders, and daily marijuana use increased significantly among all three grades. The 2010 use rates were 6.1 percent of high school seniors, 3.3 percent of 10th graders, and 1.2 percent of 8th graders compared to 2009 rates of 5.2 percent, 2.8 percent, and 1.0 percent, respectively." When the percentage of a drug of choice like marijuana use increases at the young age level of 8th grade students, about 13-years-old teens, it often means that the drug use percentage among teens will continue to rise with that group as they get older."

"Survey also showed a significant increase in the reported use of <u>MDMA, or Ecstasy</u>, with 2.4 percent of 8th graders citing past-year use, compared to 1.3 percent in 2009. Similarly, past-year MDMA use among 10th graders increased from 3.7 percent to 4.7 percent in 2010."

"<u>Binge drinking</u> continued its downward trend. Among high school seniors, 23.2 percent report having five or more drinks in a row during the past two weeks, down from 25.2 percent in 2009 and from the peak of 31.5 percent in 1998. In addition, 2010 findings showed a drop in high school seniors' past-year consumption of flavored alcoholic beverages, to 47.9 percent in 2010 from 53.4 percent in 2009. Past-year use of flavored alcohol by 8th graders was at 21.9 percent, down from 27.9 percent in 2005." I have to wonder if this is because teens are finding it harder and harder to get their hands on <u>alcohol</u> because it is regulated by the law and legal.
According to the <u>Partnership Attitude Tracking Study (PATS)</u>:

"Of those teens who reported alcohol use, a majority (62 percent) said they had their first full alcoholic drink by age 15, not including sipping or tasting alcohol. Those teens who reported alcohol use, one in four (25 percent), said they drank a full alcoholic drink for the first time by age 12 or younger. Among teens who reported <u>drinking alcohol</u>, the average age of first alcohol use was 14."

"The PATS survey also found that parents feel unprepared to respond to underage drinking by their children. Almost a third of parents (28 percent) feel "there is very little parents can do to prevent their kids from trying alcohol." One in three teens (32 percent) thinks their parents would be ok if they drank beer once in a while; yet only one in ten parents agrees with teens drinking beer at a party."

"<u>Almost half of teens (45 percent) reported they do not see a "great risk"</u> in heavy daily drinking. Only 31 percent of teens strongly disapprove of teens and peers their age getting drunk. A majority of teens, seven out of 10 (73 percent), report having <u>friends</u> who drink alcohol at least once a week."

According to the <u>2010 Dayton Area Drug Survey (DADS)</u>:

"Of the 3,049 twelfth graders surveyed, 71.8 percent reported drinking alcohol at least once in their lifetimes. Among the 55.2 percent who reported getting drunk at least once, 44.7 percent said they had done so 10 or more times. Some 26.7 percent of the respondents reported having had five or more drinks in a row on at least one occasion in the two weeks before the survey. Among the 3,753 ninth graders surveyed, 45.4 percent reported lifetime experience with alcohol. Of the 25.7 percent who had been drunk at least once, 19.7 percent had been drunk 10 or more times. Having five or more drinks in a row in the two weeks before the survey was reported by 9.1 percent. Of the 2,949 seventh graders, 22.3 percent had drunk alcohol at least once, 7.0 percent had been drunk at least once (with 8.2 percent of them drunk 10 or more times) and 2.4 percent had five or more drinks in a row in the two weeks before the survey." While the numbers aren't the same, the percentages in the DADS survey match up with the national trends.

Data from 12th grade students responding to the screening test suggests that 17.5 percent have had or currently have substance use practices indicative of drug dependence."

Mind Altering Substances: (n.) habit-forming medicinal or illicit substance, especially a narcotic.

This chapter will help you:

➢ <u>Learn tips on how to "flee from temptation"</u>

People are confronted with temptations all the time; that's how you test your inner strength. Are you able to walk away from temptation? Do you tend to live day by day instead of thinking about your entire life and how everything you do will affect the outcome of your life in one way or another? Temptation is the best feeling, for the moment. After you come to grips with yourself and realize that you don't need to fail that test in life, the better off you will be. Recognize temptations for what they are and move on. It looks like something you just have to have but then you realize that things aren't always what they seem. It can be food, gambling, shopping addiction, bad relationships or anything considered taboo that makes you feel bad but you continue to enjoy it.

➢ <u>You can learn how to say "No" to your friends</u>

Sometimes friends may want or need you to do something for them and you're not in a position to comply comfortably; however, they may mean the world to you but if you can't complete the task or whatever the request is of you – if you can't do it, say so and don't be frustrated over it. If you are able to help someone and it does not intrude on your personal life or responsibilities too much, it's great to lend a helping hand. Charity is one of the ways I give back but comfortably. If it's too stressful for me to handle, how is it good for me? Don't block your bright future before you have a chance to shine.

➢ <u>Learn the harm that mind-altering substances can do to the body</u>

Our bodies are made to take care of us for the rest of our life. Once you ingest, inhale, or poke yourself with needles, the body starts to wear down. The best way to take care of your body is to supply it with proper nutrients and exercise. There are tons of books out here and classes to discuss specifically which drug does what to a person. The main point is to understand that if you take the risk of using mind-altering substances, make sure you are aware of the harm you are risking to possibly having deadly consequences either from the substance or the environment usually involved with it. Whatever pain you may have the drugs will not solve the problem; it will only make things worse.

➢ <u>Learn how to encourage others not to go down a rocky road</u>

Life can have many curves and hills and pitfalls if you don't control yourself and your environment, as much as you respectfully can. However, if you have common sense you should be able to avoid most of the trouble. It's helpful to give positive words of encouragement to others that might not be able to see themselves out of a bad situation that you may see for them to choose a positive path. If someone approaches you to ask for advice, give them some advice if you can; if not refer them to some professional counseling. Don't gossip about other people's situations.

➢ Apply self-control at all times

Learn to mastered self-control, which may take some time depending upon the person, their environment, their genetics, and their desire to succeed in life. It depends upon you and only you. No one else can do this for you but you. We have minds and are capable of being self-reliant. When you set goals and accomplish them while staying focused; that's a form of self-control. There is no magic formula its simple science. Mastering self-control gives you freedom and peace of mind knowing that no one can anger you to distract you and make you lose control of yourself.

➢ Avoid circumstances and environments that thrive on mind-altering substances

An environment that involves the usage of mind-altering substances in order to have a good time sounds like some very boring people to associate with. Where's the ambition for life? Where's your money going? Studies show that when someone is addicted to mind-altering substances, they're usually using it to cover some sort of pain and discomfort they are experiencing.

This is all the more reason to not even try to attempt to start the habit. Illegal drugs have been around forever. It's there for you if you seek it but why waste your valuable time, money, and energy towards something that you can't be proud of. Manage your time wisely. There are plenty of things to do without involving drugs and alcohol. You had fun as a child before you knew drugs even existed.
I'm sure you can think of so many more positive things to do with your time.

➢ Learn the skills for success vs. the excuses for failure

Use your time productively in order to quickly and successfully acquire your goals to support the lifestyle you desire.

Skills to acquire for success for any situation:

1. Knowledge and preparation - know your end results.
2. Formulate your best plan in writing.
3. Take decisive action.
4. Gather and evaluate the feedback. Both positive and negative feedback.
5. Make progress by continually adapting and evolving your plans.

Understand that the skills for success are a continuous process.

Things to avoid:

1. Indecision or unclear targets.
2. No written plan – just reacting to circumstances that show up.

3. Procrastination – putting it off until later when you can do it now.
4. Become fearful due to minor set-backs and disappointments.
5. Stand still. Do the same thing (nothing) and hope for different results.

> ## Know the meaning of friends

Not only is your time very valuable, so is your time with your friends. Therefore, use your time wisely. If you have a lot of friends, meet them collectively like at a party or other major events. If you have two or three good buddies, I suggest you manage your time with each of them closely so you can enjoy your time and friendship with them but also complete the other things that are required and necessary for you to enjoy your life and lifestyle blissfully. True friends understand when you need to take care of your responsibilities. If they can't respect and understand your priorities, they're not your friends.

> ## Live a healthy lifestyle

You have to live inside of your body throughout your lifetime. Therefore, it only makes sense to take care of it every single day internally and externally. Some people will take care of their material possessions much better than themselves. Living a healthy lifestyle means waking up every day full of expectation for greatness, not dreading the sunlight and hating everyone in sight. If you're not enjoying life, you have yet to discover your purpose in life.

> ## Learn to live a conscious free life

There are so many opportunities out here to succeed in life that you don't need to think in a cheap manner and do things illegally to have all of your desires met. Don't settle for less in life. Live your life! Enjoy all of the blessings you have and prepare for all of the unexpected blessings. If you expect great things and work towards them, you will receive the results from your persistence. Your dreams might not happen exactly the way you want them to but if you're on the right track and staying positive and focused, your breakthrough is guaranteed! You should look forward to each new day filled with exciting new adventures and learning opportunities to better yourself and assisting others along the way. If your life is unhappy, you don't have to stay like that. Pinpoint what is correct and what is not correct with your specific situation(s) and try to resolve what's keeping you from your total freedom of expression.

SELF – ANALYSIS
Assessment

Chapter 8

1. What are your biggest fears? How will you flee from temptation?

    _____
    _____
    _____
    _____
    _____

2. Have you ever experienced situations where you wished you said "no" instead of "yes?"

    _____
    _____
    _____
    _____
    _____

3. How would you encourage someone close to you to quit using drugs?

    _____
    _____
    _____
    _____
    _____

4. How do you tell someone that you're not interested in destroying your body internally and mentally, even though they're your friend and you might appear to be "lame?"

    _____
    _____
    _____
    _____
    _____

5. What are your friends' names and what makes them so special?

_____
_____
_____
_____
_____

6. What are ways to avoid people that you know are no good for you to associate with?

_____
_____
_____
_____
_____

7. What challenges are keeping you from living a healthy lifestyle?

_____
_____
_____
_____
_____

8. What, if anything, will you truly miss if you choose to live a productive life that makes you work towards a positive and prosperous future?

_____
_____
_____
_____
_____

9. What are your setbacks in life?

_____
_____
_____
_____
_____

10. Identify your triggers for negativity and explain how you can control them.

_____

_____

_____

_____

_____

Notes:

Chapter Nine:

Employee v. Self Employed:

Chapter Summary:
This chapter is designed to teach you how to determine if you want to become an employee or self-employed. You learn through your choices what works best for you and your vision of success. Should you fill out a resume or a business plan or both? It's important to know what fit fits you best. My program was created to teach you the importance of making good decisions, while still being able to maintain a fulfilling lifestyle. Once you have made your decision, it is good to seek legal advice also to approve you're making the best decision for you and your family.

Statistics Show: The majority of the people that work, work for someone else.

Employee: (n.) A person working for another person or a business firm for pay.

Self-Employed: (adj.) Earning one's living directly from one's own profession or business, as a freelance writer or artist, rather than as an employee earning salary or commission from another.

This chapter will help you:

➢ <u>Learn about resources that provide you with information on how to get started</u>

Technology today has made the world so much closer so much faster! With this great influx of information, try to take advantage of what the internet and the world have to offer. The library will always have a plethora of resourceful information to explain any and everything you need answered.

Websites that can assist you during your research:

- Search engines such as Ask.com, Dogpile.com, and Google.com are useful
- Dictionary.com and Reference.com
- SBA.gov (free small business advice)
- Score.gov (free business counseling advice)
- IRS.gov (tax related information)
- Entreprenuer.com (business related topics)
- About.com (various topics are discussed)
- eHow.com (free tutorial videos)
- CDC.gov (environmental research and stats)
- Docstoc.com (free templates and examples of documents for business)
- SOS.gov (secretary of state – file with the state you currently reside in order to incorporate your business)

➤ Determine if you were meant to be an employee or self-employed

Do you like structured environments where you're given a set of instructions and you complete the task(s) and receive a set salary on a regularly scheduled payment plan? Or do you like to take risks in life and believe that you can create regular streams of revenue to support yourself and your lifestyle without impending upon others?

Working as an employee can have many rewards. You know your responsibilities and you have a comfortable way to support yourself. You can assist a great cause or assist the weak or whatever you are doing to earn a living working for someone, or a big corporation like the government, there are great benefits. In some cases, you can receive packages for savings, medical, and dental benefits to assist you while you are working for their company. You can retire knowing you have your income set for the golden years.

Being self-employed is an option for people who are risk takers. They don't mind taking a risk with the skills they have obtained to seek a way to provide for themselves independently. They have the option of being a sole proprietor, an independent contractor, a company, or a corporation. The bigger the project, the more people involved and you should consider hiring or outsourcing if your business is too demanding for one person alone.

Knowledge of particular skills that's wanted or needed in society to support yourself financially along with a passion to succeed is what's needed to succeed professionally in any area of life as an employee or self-employed. Passion is needed because you will definitely have bumps in the road and will need to remember why you are working so diligently towards your goal whatever it may be.

➤ Fill out an application and resume

When filling out an application you are telling the potential employer that you feel you meet their standards and are employable and a good match for their company. If you have never filled out an application before this is good practice for you to see what answers you need to generally know. Also, if you have never worked before, you must rely upon your skills you have gained over time even if you were not paid for them. Have you ever volunteered to assist a person or a company or foundation? What have you done to help others? A potential employer is looking at your job application for key information: any knowledge, skills, and/or experience that will help them grow their business. Employers pay you to ensure that they will receive more business and money because they are investing in you by hiring you. Therefore, thoroughly research a company before you seek possible employment with them to ensure a good match.

Sample - Job Application Form

Instructions: Print clearly in black or blue ink. Answer all questions. Sign and date the form.

PERSONAL INFORMATION:

First Name _____

Middle Name _____

Last Name _____

Street Address

_____

City, State, Zip Code

_____

Phone Number

(____)_____

Are you eligible to work in the United States?

Yes _____ No _____

If you are under age 18, do you have an employment/age certificate?

Yes ___ No ___

Have you been convicted of or pleaded no contest to a felony within the last five years?

Yes _____ No _____

If yes, please explain: _____

_____

POSITION/AVAILABILITY:

Position Applied For

_____

Days/Hours Available

Monday _____
Tuesday _____
Wednesday _____
Thursday _____
Friday _____
Saturday _____
Sunday _____

Hours Available: from _____ to _____

What date are you available to start work?

_____

EDUCATION:

Name and Address of School - Degree/Diploma - Graduation Date

_____

_____

_____

_____

_____

Skills and Qualifications: Licenses, Skills, Training, Awards

_____

_____

EMPLOYMENT HISTORY:

Present Or Last Position:

Employer: _____

Address:_____ _____

Supervisor: _____

Phone: _____

Email: _____ _____

Position Title: _____

From: _____To: _____

Responsibilities: _____

_____

Salary: _____

Reason for Leaving: _____

==========

Previous Position:

Employer: _____

Address:_____ _____

Supervisor: _____

Phone: _____

Email: _____

Position Title: _____

From: _____ To: _____

Responsibilities: _____

_____

Salary: _____

Reason for Leaving: _____

May We Contact Your Present Employer?

Yes _____ No _____

References:

Name/Title Address Phone

_____

_____

_____

I certify that information contained in this application is true and complete. I understand that false information may be grounds for not hiring me or for immediate termination of employment at any point in the future if I am hired. I authorize the verification of any or all information listed above.

Signature_____

Date_____

> Strategies to build or improve your speaking skills

When someone hears you speak, what do you want them to hear? Do you have a calm, screechy, or raspy voice? People receive all kinds of signals from your body language and your voice when you speak. In order to convey confidence and self-assurance, you must first collect your thoughts and know what you're going to say. Then, speak clearly and communicate effectively. You want the other person to understand what you are expressing to them.

Great tips for speaking:

- Know the subject discussed – Get organized

- Create an outline

- Rehearse over and over and over

- Dress for success

- Master your body language

- Deliver your message or speech with confidence

- Always have a pleasant personality

- Know that the listeners actually heard your message

> Understand the importance of writing out a business plan for entrepreneurs

A business plan is your road map to prepare and assist you in achieving your goals in a well-planned thought-out strategy for success. If you are serious about business and want to support yourself financially with ease and create your destiny, it is better to be as prepared as possible.

What's the basic information needed to have a successful business?

- Start with an idea

- Does it have any value?

- Find a need for your idea

- Write a business plan

- Establish a business license

- Market your business

- Advertise your business

- Create repeat customers with your product(s) or service(s)

What's your idea of a great business or service? Will enough people need this to make their lives easier or will they have fun with your product or service? The best business to create is one in which people need what you have to offer. That way you will always be needed by your customers. You must learn how to establish a simple business plan.

Simple Business Plan Outline Terms:

1. **Executive Summary**: Write this last. It's just a page or two of highlights.

2. **Company Description**: Legal establishment, history, start-up-plans, etc.

3. **Product or Service**: Describe what you're selling. Focus on customer benefits.

4. **Market Analysis**: You need to know your market, customer needs, where they are, how to reach them, etc.

5. **Strategy and Implementation**: Be specific. Include management responsibilities with dates and budgets. Make sure you can track results.

5. **Web Plan Summary**: For e-commerce, include discussion of website, development costs, operations, sales and marketing strategies.

6. **Management Team**: Describe the organization and the key management team members.

7. **Financial Analysis**: Make sure to include at the very least your projected Profit and Loss tables.

➢ <u>Market and advertise yourself and your business</u>

I love marketing and advertising! If people don't know you exist, they can't respond to you and purchase your products and/or services. Now, hopefully you want to appeal to them favorably instead of annoying them, but my point is that if you aren't seen or heard, how do people know you exist? Marketing and advertising take an investment to get started such as creating your business cards with your name, business name (and address if not an internet-based business), telephone number, and website information on there in order to show someone you are a legal entity and they have something they can keep and refer to when they're looking to spend money with someone like you and your business. Your business should be something that people need and not necessarily want unless that want is a strong temptation and they can't resist. Then, you have a great concept and should do well financially.

Marketing tips:

- What's your action plan? (What will be done? How will it be done?)

- What's your target market? (Who are your specific customers: kids, pets, stores?)

- Know how to describe your competition.

- Explain their strengths and weaknesses and why you're better.

- How does your business influence society? (Do you donate/give back)

- What's your measurable outcome? It needs to be specific to have meaning.

- Forecast your budget: expected costs of production, distribution, and marketing.

- Create customer loyalty.

> ## Brand your reputation

What makes your business unique? If I close my eyes and hear one of my favorite singers or voiccovers, I know who it is because they are unique and that's why they are so popular. If you think you have something unique and can stand the test of time, put it to the test. Guard your master plan and get opinions from friends, family, and potential customers. If you have a great rate of success, then go for it! The world needs to know about your product and/or services.

> ## Understand the art of negotiation

There's your side, their side, and the truth to every situation. The art of negotiation is to come out of any meeting knowing that you received the best outcome and the other party is satisfied as well. You want to be sure that you are well prepared for any meeting and establish clearly what you are expecting in return for what you are willing to give. Make sure that you know what you're willing to accept and will definitely refuse.

Things you should establish:

- Research - Be well prepared.

- Listen carefully to what the other side needs to be satisfied.

- Put things in writing.

- Don't assume anything.

- Pay attention to body language.

- Be prepared to walk away.

- Be prepared for the other side to walk away.

- Become a great closer. Seal the deal.

SELF – ANALYSIS
Assessment

Chapter 9

1. What books or reference material is needed for you to complete your goals?

   _____

   _____

   _____

   _____

   _____

2. Are you more prone to be an employee or self-employed? Explain.

   _____

   _____

   _____

   _____

   _____

3. What specific skills are needed for you to accomplish your goals?

   _____

   _____

   _____

   _____

   _____

4. What are some of the skills and talents you can explain about yourself for a job interview as to why you should be hired?

   _____

   _____

   _____

   _____

   _____

5. What are some of the necessities to complete before you start your own business?

_____
_____
_____
_____
_____

6. What are some of the positive adjectives you can use to explain who you are?

_____
_____
_____
_____
_____

7. What are some ways you can promote your business?

_____
_____
_____
_____
_____

8. What are other positive characteristics you would like to add to your reputation?

_____
_____
_____
_____
_____

Notes:

Chapter Ten:

The Life of a True Diva:

Chapter Summary:
This chapter is designed to show you how you can live the life of a Diva for life! This chapter combines questionnaires and essay problems for you to assess and determine if you have learned what it takes to be a true *Diva*. You will learn how to set the pace for your life with a high self-esteem and maintain it in a classy, professional, and fun way for the future while helping others along the way.

Statistics Show: True Divas are developed from within first.

Diva: (n.) A glamorous and successful female performer or personality.

This Chapter will help you:

➤ Love yourself unconditionally

You can depend upon yourself more than you can from anyone else especially as you mature in age. Take a look in the mirror and ask yourself, "What's not to love?" Of course you realize that no person has a "perfect" body without surgery, which really still isn't perfect because it's not real.

Loving yourself means that you will love yourself for who you are, and who you aren't, underneath it all. Every day you need to be reminded how much you love yourself. Appreciate the specific things about you that separate you from everyone else and make you special. Forget the past, you can't change it, but you can learn from it and improve yourself. Learn to heal yourself from guilt because you should understand that everything in life will not go your way; life does not do that for any one. Situations will come and you will have to deal with them; and that should make you stronger.

➤ Articulate proficiently

A true Diva must be able to articulate proficiently while explaining herself at all times. You should be able to express yourself clearly and with a calm manner no matter what the situation. The best way to make that possible is to know as much as possible about the chosen topic; therefore, when you speak, you know what you're saying. If you don't know, don't make excuses for not knowing. No one knows everything. Be willing to learn something new if the environment grants you that opportunity.

➤ Walk with confidence

Every day we walk to get to and from our destinations. Now, observe how you're walking while you're in route to your destination. Do you appear clumsy, graceful, or not sure what you're doing? Your walk gives people around you an impression of you without you even speaking your first word. Observe people who you admire and notice their gait or the way they walk. What does their body language say to you? What do you want others to think of you by observation? Standing tall not only gives the appearance of confidence but it is also the correct posture to have for proper bone growth and structure.

> Remain poised at all times

A true Diva never lets someone see her sweat! Remember to practice deep breathing techniques to remain calm at all times. Take a moment to step back and collect your thoughts. Count to ten. Try not to make major decisions while your heart is pumping at a fast rate of speed, unless you're on a game show.

> Understand the importance of personal-quality time

The world can steal your time if you allow it to do so. Remember that your time is precious and you want to be able to feel good about what you're doing ALL the time. Your valuable personal time should be spent wisely. Quality time can be spent with the family and loved ones doing special things together. Cherish these moments in time. Helping others is a great way to use your spare time wisely while helping society collectively. This time is very vital to balancing your life.

> Strategies to build or improve your self-esteem

In order to build or improve your self-esteem, you must first learn to love yourself. You are a beautiful person created by our Creator specifically to serve a unique purpose. What is your purpose in life? What do you enjoy doing most? Love to look in the mirror every day and see something great about yourself. You can do this while you're brushing your teeth.

Understanding that life is full of surprises and unexpected situations; learn to bounce off of those situations because you are not those situations. You (your soul) are an observer of the situations. The choices you decide to take in life will strongly determine the type of lifestyle you will live. Let go of guilt; there's no need to hold on to extra negative mental luggage; it wears down on your self-esteem.

Lastly, learn to accept someone's compliment towards you. If someone took the time to compliment you respect them by thanking them for their kind words and move on. If someone compliments you that does not mean that they want to spend the rest of their life with you, they are simply expressing positive words to help brighten your day.

➢ <u>The art of being feminine</u>

The beauty of being a woman! It's truly a blessing to have men, women, and children adorn you just because you're a woman. Now, to take it even further, knowing we bring life into the world and provide love and loving situations and nurture life is a great blessing. We run the world!

➢ <u>Walk the catwalk of life with determination</u>

Do you know that no one absolutely knows exactly everything to do in life! No matter whom you are, no matter what amount of knowledge or connections you have, life is not promised to you on top of a Diva platter. That should not stop you from accomplishing your goals in life and being the best that you can be. If you live your life to the fullest, what excuses will you use to keep you from accomplishing your goals?

There are a lot of people that really think they want the best for themselves but refuse to take the first step towards success. Don't just think about it, do what's necessary to accomplish your goals and your life will be successful because you created your own destiny. When I learned how to set goals and accomplish them (graduating from college, raising a loving family, creating a successful business, losing over 50 pounds, consulting, etc.), there isn't anything or anyone that can stop me from being successful in life! When you determine what your destiny is don't let anyone else deter you. This is what Divas are made of!

SELF – ANALYSIS
Assessment

Chapter 10

➤ <u>Develop the Diva within</u>

1. Explain the difference between the mind, body, and soul.

   _____
   _____
   _____
   _____
   _____
   _____

2. How do you feel about yourself currently?

   _____
   _____
   _____
   _____
   _____
   _____

3. What improvements can you make with yourself?

   _____
   _____
   _____
   _____
   _____

4. How should you present yourself at all times?

   _____
   _____
   _____
   _____
   _____
   _____

5. What does your nonverbal language say to others?

_____

_____

_____

_____

_____

6. What separates you from others?

_____

_____

_____

_____

_____

7. How do you speak with confidence?

_____

_____

_____

_____

_____

8. How do handle bullies?

_____

_____

_____

_____

_____

9. How do you handle stressful situations?

_____

_____

_____

_____

_____

10. How do you relax?

_____
_____
_____
_____
_____

11. What's the best way to handle your Haters?

_____
_____
_____
_____
_____

12. What's the best way to handle peer pressure?

_____
_____
_____
_____
_____

13. How do you resist temptations?

_____
_____
_____
_____
_____

14. Explain your usual exercise routine.

_____
_____
_____
_____
_____

15. Are you more inclined to be an employee or self-employed?

_____
_____
_____
_____
_____

16. How do you contribute to society?

_____
_____
_____
_____
_____

17. What will your branding be?

_____
_____
_____
_____
_____

18. What does it take to be a Diva? Express yourself.

_____
_____
_____
_____
_____

19. What are some of the ways you have accepted who you are, even though you're not perfect?

_____
_____
_____
_____
_____

20. What difference, if any, have you noticed while practicing how to walk, sit, and stand taller?

_____

_____

_____

_____

_____

21. Do you like personal quality time? Does it matter to you?

_____

_____

_____

_____

_____

22. How do you work on your self-esteem daily?

_____

_____

_____

_____

_____

23. What challenges do you face that you are not able to overcome? Explain.

_____

_____

_____

_____

24. What are some professional advisors in your community that can assist you should you ever need additional resourceful information? (Score.gov)

_____

_____

_____

_____

Pledge for Success

I Promise To:

- Love God and pray for understanding

- Love myself

- Have love for mankind

- Learn to be responsible for me

- Stay disciplined

- Let go of the past and move forward

- Ignore negative thoughts that's self-debilitating

- Ignore ignorance

- Control my emotions

- Assist others in need, that I can comfortably assist

- Choose my *friends* carefully

- Determine that the source of my happiness lies within me

- Determine my financial freedom

- Remember that Image Is Everything!

Studio Steffanie
modeling & entertainment agency
······················"**Image Is Everything**"······················
Modeling Workshops What does your image say about you?

For More Info www.**StudioSteffanie**.com or **678.330.8139**

StudioSteffanie Agency

Certifies that

_____
(Insert your Name Here)

Has completed the required hours necessary to officially become a

DIVA

 Ms. Steffanie Haggins
President StudioSteffanie Agency

Contact and Other Important Information

Mailing Address:
Steffanie Haggins, Wellness Coach
863 Flat Shoals Rd., #139
Conyers, GA 30094

Other Correspondence:
Phone: 678-330-8139
Email: StudioSteffanie@gmail.com
Website: www.StudioSteffanie.com

Open to speak to individuals from primary school though adulthood, college students, entrepreneurs, individuals, groups, companies or businesses, those with little knowledge, and those with much, those thinking of starting a business, or those just interested in learning skills to build and maintain your image and wealth financially, mentally, and spiritually.

Speaking Engagements:

Panel Speaker   Negotiated Fee + Accommodations
Featured Speaker   Negotiated Fee + Accommodations

"Image Is Everything!"
Workbook

"Steffanie Haggins is devoted to helping young women make better choices in life with loving, creative energy and a strong-minded commitment. I have been very impressed, as well as touched with the joy Steffanie expresses sharing valuable principles to young women. She is a mentor, a sister, a friend… I am sure you will find her book inspirational, fun, and instructional. Steffanie Haggins who is a beautiful woman can help younger beautiful women realize their beauty, too. You will be blessed by reading this book."

*The Legendary Actress, Ms. Alison Newman-Mills (Played in **Julia** with Dianne Carroll)*

"When you think of up-beat, StudioSteffanie should be the poster child! She is one of the most positive thinking and action oriented people I know. She's always a pleasure to work with and her up-beat attitude towards life is infectious!"

Bill E. Leavell
Former Director of DeKalb's Office of Arts, Culture, & Entertainment
Executive Director Porter Sanford Performing Arts & Community Center

"StudioSteffanie is an Amazing trailblazing leader. She has remained committed to working to empower youth in an effort to ensure that they are equipped with the tools needed to excel in life and to maximize their potential. Steffanie is an inspiration to all who are blessed with the privilege of being in her presence. StudioSteffanie Rocks!"

Bernada Nicole Baker, MBA. MPH, MDiv
President & CEO of the Princess within Foundation

Made in the USA
Middletown, DE
17 March 2022

62717557R00057